Chipped Dishes, Zippers, & Prayer

Meditations for Women

Chipped Dishes, Zippers, & Prayer

Ruth Gibson

Vitality Press
a division of Wheaton Counseling Associates, Ltd.
Wheaton, IL
(630) 668-3331
Books may be ordered from the author

CHIPPED DISHES, ZIPPERS, & PRAYER

Original Copyright ©1977 by Word, Inc.
Copyright © 1981 by Ruth Gibson
All rights reserved.
No part of this book may be reproduced
in any form, except for brief quotations
in reviews, without the written permission
of the author.

Illustrations by Dennis Hill.

ISBN 0-8499-2808-7
Library of Congress catalog card number: 77-76350
Printed in the United States of America

First Printing, September 1977
Second Printing, March 1978
Third Printing, May 1978
Fourth Printing, November 1981
Fifth Printing, September 1985
Sixth Printing, February 1997

In remembrance of
Jesus
whose mother never went to college

Contents

On Being Alone	11
On Communion	13
On a Dryer That Naps	14
On Coming Home Late from Nursery School	15
On Enthusiasm	16
On Conversational Prayer	17
On Buying Oxfords	18
On Varnishing Cupboards	20
On Mothers-in-Law	22
On Rice and Milk	24
On Moving	25
On Old Shoes	26
On Eating Lunch with an Octogenarian	27

On a Baby Girl	28
On Memories of the LaSalle Street Station	29
On Eating at McDonald's	31
On Violin Music	32
On Daydreaming About a New Couch	33
On Playing Peekaboo	35
On Vulnerability	37
On Christmas	38
On Chipped Dishes	40
On an Industrial Arts Teacher	42
On Beauty	43
On Boys in the Living Room	45
On *Song of the South*	46
On Waiting in the Doctor's Office	47
On Different Lifestyles	48
On Old Newspapers	50
On a Rusty Bumper	52
On Zippers	53
On a Funeral	54
On Valentine's Day	55
On Three in a Bedroom	56
On Guna the Guinea Pig	57
On Husbands Who Stay Late at the Office	59
On a Hole in the Ceiling	61
On a Thirty-fifth Wedding Anniversary	63
On Past and Future	64
On Being an Optimist or a Complainer	65

On Desk Work	67
On April Fool's Day	68
On BankAmericard	69
On Going to Graduate School	70
On Quitting Graduate School	71
On Senility	72
On Waiting My Turn	73
On Homemade Limpa Bread	74
On Bike Riding and Jealousy	76
On Listening	78
On Old-Timers	80
On Buying a House	81
On the Salt of the Earth	83
On Learning from Mistakes	85
On an Escaped Hamster	86
On Babies Who Grow Up	87
On a Box of Kleenex	89
On Monster Mutant Bikes	90
On Old Hymns	92
On Becoming Thirty-nine	93

On Being Alone

Today I'm alone in a cabin in Canada. My family is out fishing in a boat that's "a little too small for five fishermen." Being the fifth fisherman is like being the fifth wheel on the wagon.

Usually I bring a whole library of reading material on vacations, but this time I didn't bring enough, assuming the fish would occupy all my time. There's not much housekeeping to do in this little cabin. I've read every matchbook, map, and fishing magazine. This is my moment of truth.

Dear God, I'm sitting here with my Bible, a ball-point pen, and a spiral notebook. For years I've talked about being a writer and have gone to numerous writer's conferences. If you want me to be a writer, please teach me from the little everyday things and show me how you fit into my life. Teach me your truths. In memory of the one who spent forty days and forty nights alone in the wilderness. Amen.

On Communion

Today we ate lunch in a small restaurant while traveling home. My husband and I had fish and chips, while the children had grilled cheese sandwiches and hamburgers. My husband took the small plain roll from his plate, broke it into pieces and passed it to each family member, as he said, "This is the body of Jesus, given for you. Eat in remembrance of him."

Dear Jesus, you know how much we care about nourishing our bodies. In your wisdom, you told us to think of you each time we eat. Forgive us for waiting for formal passing of the cup and breaking of bread to remember you. Thank you for a husband who understands what you were teaching us. In memory of the one who used simple things in life to help us glimpse the profound. Amen.

On a Dryer That Naps

I've done six loads of wash today since we just returned from vacation yesterday. The ten-year-old dryer is acting very human because after each load it drys, it needs to rest an hour before drying another. This has happened before and has something to do with the dryer getting overheated.

Dear Heavenly Father, thank you for clotheslines and clothespins. Help me not to feel resentful for that tiny bit of extra effort it takes to put clothes on the line. My Mother always says it's so much fun to "hang out." Help me to learn these simple pleasures. In memory of Jesus and his disciples who had no electrical appliances but still had time to do their most important work. Amen.

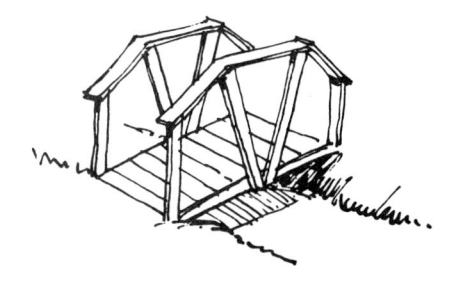

On Coming Home Late from Nursery School

David was late coming home from nursery school. The neighbor was taking a turn at driving, and I was waiting for him to walk from their yard to ours, over the little white bridge over the creek in the back yard.

I did the dishes while I waited, looking out the window at the little white bridge. After fifteen minutes which seemed like forever, he finally came.

Dear God, thank you for nursery schools. Thank you even more for the glorious moment four year olds are back in their mommies' arms. Thank you for dishes to be done. The waiting would be harder without the work. In memory of him who has waited a long time for his children to come home. Amen.

On Enthusiasm

I just talked to some friends who are coming over on Saturday. This will be a real reunion. That's my idea of a good time. Since hanging up the phone a minute ago, I feel so enthusiastic I think I could paint a house, climb a mountain, or write a book.

Lord, you know how turned on I get to people and the anticipation of being with friends. You also know the other side of me which is lazy and slow and could sleep half a day. Two things I pray: that there be less of the tired, weary me and more of the enthusiastic me; that my excitement and enthusiasm might flow over to a love for your written word, and that I might feel as excited talking to you as to an old high school friend. In the name of him who created all of the things and people I'm excited about. Amen.

Dear God, thank you for parents who didn't criticize me for changing my mind. They didn't say, "You'll never learn to make up your mind." I appreciate not hearing predictions like that. In memory of the one who guides parents in their most important job. Amen.

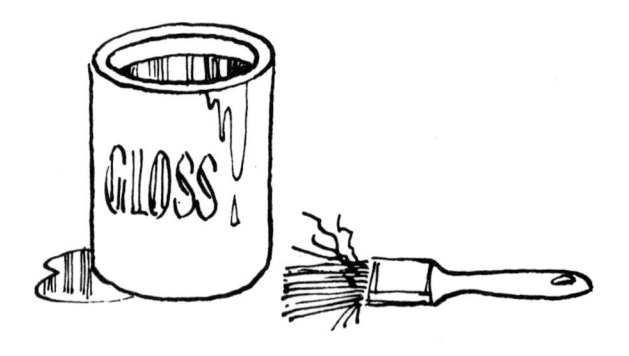

On Varnishing Cupboards

Today I varnished some cupboards, and the bristles of the brush came off on the varnished surface. I was mad. It took a long time to pick off the bristles and doubled the time of the job. I took the brush back to the man in the hardware store and told him about the miserable performance of the brush that he had recommended. He showed me how I should have bent it back and forth to get those loose bristles out before I started. Disgustedly, I told him he should have told me that in the first place.

Dear Jesus, I remember now that you went to Calvary's cross for me and that man. Please let me see every sales clerk through your eyes. Let me never walk into a store without remembering that clerks have their own hassles.

On Conversational Prayer

Tonight we had a potluck supper and Bible Study for teenagers. These thirty high school friends feel at ease with each other and at home with my family. We introduced the idea of conversational prayer to teach them that God is able to hear our everyday problems in our everyday voices. Our three little preschool boys sat on the floor among us, curled up in the laps of their teenaged friends.

Dear God, thank you for the special time tonight. Some of the high school kids said they learned that prayer was very simple and real, and that they could be a part of it. They learned that even they could pray when they heard our two year old join in with his own simple words to you. In memory of the one who said that little children were a part of the Kingdom of Heaven. Amen.

On Buying Oxfords

While shopping for shoes for my boys I am remembering when I was a four year old, and my Mom and Dad took me shopping for shoes. I picked out some tan and brown oxfords that were satisfactory to me and my folks. While wrapping the shoes, the salesman said, "Yes, these are fine shoes, suitable for either a little boy or girl."

With great indignation I said, "I don't want those shoes if they could be worn by some boy." The poor salesman had obviously said too much and lost a sale.

While leaving the store, I remember the other family members had their new shoes and I had none. I was confused and sorry for what I had said. In my fickle, preschool heart, I knew I really wanted those shoes. When we got home, I spilled out my whole sad story about how I was sorry I couldn't make up my mind and could I please have those brown and tan shoes after all?

They need to know of your love first. My complaints can only be acceptable when delivered in a more appropriate way. Teach me your way of doing things. Amen.

On Mothers-in-Law

I just heard another mother-in-law joke. Anger and uneasiness settle in when I hear jokes like that or snide remarks like, "My mother-in-law is coming. How will I ever live through it?"

I'm angry because the complainer is criticizing the very one who produced her spouse. If that lady's mother-in-law is so bad, how can her son be lovable?

I feel uneasy because I hope to be a "mother-in-law" someday, and I don't want to commit all those heinous crimes attributed to them.

Dear God, thank you for my mother-in-law who is also a friend. Thank you that she took time for feeding, diaper changing and nose wiping. Thank you that she knew the business of building a man and then she knew how to let go of him. Thank you for that moral training she gave to the little boy who became my husband. I pray today for the little girls who will be my daughters-in-law. Help their moms to raise them well. Help me to give them solid, grown men, trained in the way they should go. In memory of him who established the training rules. Amen.

On Rice and Milk

Tonight we had rice and milk for supper. We fed the family for about fifty cents and put the two dollars saved into a fund for the hungry. We do this almost every Sunday night.

O God, don't let me think my small donation is so great or that my sacrifice really gives me empathy for the starving. I don't know what to do to help. I'm frustrated by the immensity of the hunger problem. Please show me how I should live and eat, and please provide for the hungry people even as you did the five thousand. Amen.

On Moving

Today we moved. Neighbors came in and cleaned the house after we were gone. The new people came in and found the neighbors just leaving the spic-and-span house.

Dear God, thank you for neighbors who would clean a house after I am gone and am too far away to thank them in person. Let them show your love to the new people as they did to me. Please continue to dwell in that house with them as you did with us. In memory of him who gave those neighbors a love greater than man's love. Amen.

On Old Shoes

Today in church the pastor asked for old shoes to be brought in for people in the city who needed them. In the afternoon, we brought a grocery bag of shoes to the pastor's office. The floor was so covered with sacks of shoes, there was no room to walk.

Dear God, thank you for a church that responds to needs. Please walk with the people who wear those shoes. Let them know they are loved by you. Use us in simple ways, as agents of your love. In memory of him who did a lot of walking with just sandals on his feet. Amen.

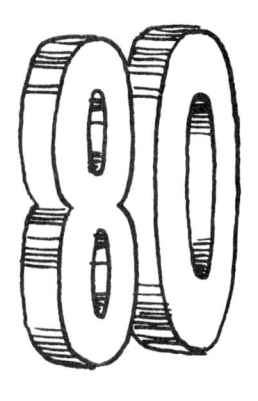

On Eating Lunch with an Octogenarian

Today I went to lunch with a lady who is in her eighties. She has had over forty years more experience than I. We talked of many things we have in common. Mostly she shared her memories, both happy and sad, of days when her family was young—the good old days.

Dear God, thank you for octogenarians who are willing to spend time with me, when I'm so much younger and know so much less. Let me always remember how much elderly people have to offer. Remind me often that they just might enjoy lunch with me, and that only you know how few lunches are left for me to enjoy with them. In memory of him who loved both young and old. Amen.

Not Another One!

On a Baby Girl

My friends had a girl when they wanted a boy. They told everyone that they were counting on two of each, and bemoaned the fact that now they had three girls and only one boy. They talked often about this "mistake" even after the little girl could talk and understand.

Dear God, please help me not to judge others, but I feel such pain for that little girl when she hears that she's not quite what they wanted. Thank you for all healthy babies and my three precious sons. Show me my blind spots, where I may be hurting someone else with thoughtless words I've said. In memory of him who was rejected by the crowds in Jerusalem. Amen.

On Memories of the LaSalle Street Station

I got off the train at the LaSalle Street station in Chicago. I was just a little kid because I remember the men were carrying their brief cases at my eye level. All I could see were the dull colors of men's topcoats and briefcases. The crowd was moving fast, so I thought I'd just hang on to my dad's coat. My feet did double time to keep up with the commuter stampede into the main part of the station.

When we got into the depot, I was startled to see my dad carefully watching the crowd, looking for me. Quickly my eyes traveled up the coat I was hanging on to, and I saw that I had been holding on to a total stranger. I was embarrassed and so relieved to get back to my dad.

Dear Heavenly Father, forgive me for often forgetting to look up and make sure it's really you I'm following. I often get swept along in crowds, then realize you are waiting lovingly and patiently for me to get back in a right relationship with you. Thank you for a dad who taught me what you're like. In memory of the one whose robe was clutched by little children. Amen.

On Daydreaming About a New Couch

I'm daydreaming about a new couch and shelves in the living room. How easy it is to spend time *wanting* things, when there are people with heavy needs all around.

O God, please help me to put love into action on people. You know I spend an awesome amount of time putting my covetousness into action on material things. I want to be free of materialism that chokes me on every corner of suburbia, but on the other hand, I don't want my home to be so shabby that it's dishonoring to you. Help me to know the difference between furniture that is comfortable and just plain threadbare. Show me the difference between showiness and good taste. Let my home be furnished in love and hospitality. Let it be given to sharing and good fellowship.

I pray that people will remember that you are here. Let my furnishings not detract, but only add to the love and happiness in my home. In the memory of him who was born in a stable. Amen.

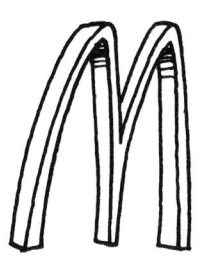

On Eating at McDonald's

A haggard young couple was eating with three squirming kids across from us at McDonald's today. The little four-year-old boy was whining to his mother that he wanted an orange drink. The mother told him to "Be quiet, or I'll give you something to cry about."

Dear Father, be very close to weary moms and dads who are at their wits' end. Give us your wisdom when we speak and your love when we act. Let us hear the needs, both real and whimsical, of those little ones with tears staining precious little faces. Amen.

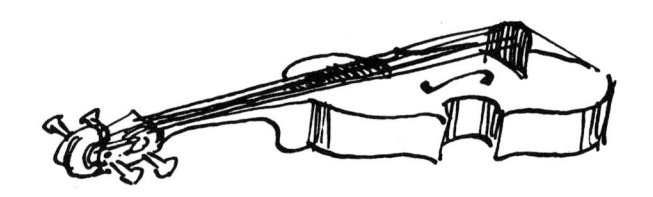

On Violin Music

Tonight I went to a banquet where a friend played the violin. Hearing him play some old familiar hymns provided an exquisite worship experience.

Dear God, it seemed like the doors of heaven were opened while I heard that music. Thank you for the violin player and the talent that made possible those moments of worship. While I listened to that music I felt like I was born again. In memory of Jesus who said to Nicodemus, "Ye must be born again." Amen.

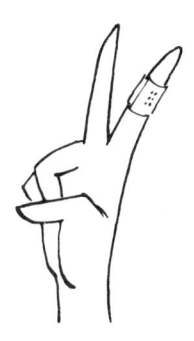

On Vulnerability

Today I'm battling with vulnerability. Some of my Christian friends speak so much of weakness, I wonder where the victory is. On the other hand, many people I know appear to "have their game together" in such a fine way that they are apparently beyond reach.

I sit here somewhere in the middle, aware that I could fill either role—failure or success.

Dear Heavenly Father, only you can sort out these musings. You are the King of Kings, so I know you want quality in my life. Yet, you are my Savior, and I need to be redeemed from my sinful ways. Let me be honest, Lord, and remember both of these amazing truths: I am a sinner saved by grace, and I serve the creator of the universe! In his holy name, Amen.

On Christmas

Profound philosophical thoughts seem to come to me in lines —waiting lines, that is, in post offices, at railroad crossings, in libraries, at ticket booths, and here in the supermarket where I am now. It's Christmas time and the ceilings are covered with crepe paper. It's festooned like a junior prom, except the colors are red and green. The rack in front of me is filled with plastic candy canes stuffed with sugar-coated chocolate pellets. "Rudolph's nose is still red and shiny," I'm reminded by *loud* loudspeakers.

Something inside me screams and cries, "What's this got to do with Bethlehem?" I imagine myself up on the check-out counter shouting, "Hold it! None of you know what this is all about!"

Dear Jesus, you know I won't get on the counter and shout that it is your birthday. But how can I gently show the world the Incarnation? Please make me aware of what I do at Christmas that might be leaving you out. Help me to begin with my own family that I may help them to find you reborn in their hearts. In memory of the baby who was born before Pampers were invented. Amen.

On Chipped Dishes

The towels are frayed. The dishes are chipped. The sheets have holes. The furniture sags. After sixteen years of marriage, all those beautiful wedding gifts look like they've seen their best days.

Perhaps it's good that these things are old and tarnished. If they always stayed like new it would be easy to think that happiness or lasting values are in *things*. It's clear to me as I look around that there is more to life than all this baggage.

Lord, thank you for the clothes, furniture, books, and appliances. The things I have would seem like riches to so many in the world. Forgive me for not appreciating them more. Lead me to a balance of being grateful for your provisions, and yet not coveting more or better things. Let my belongings not become idols, but let me be a good steward of what I have. In memory of him who taught us to share what we have with others. Amen.

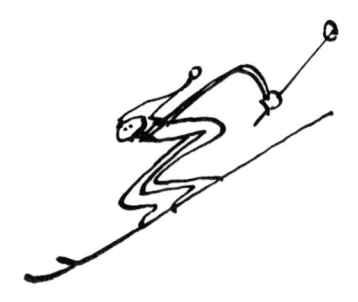

On an Industrial Arts Teacher

"He likes snow skiing, model rocketry and model cars. He has cool posters and such a neat class room." My son is raving about his fantastic Industrial Arts teacher. He has spent the last twenty minutes with his eyes sparkling with enthusiasm as he exudes about this teacher and the great way he teaches.

Dear Lord, thank you for this teacher who finds so much joy in his work. Be close to him and keep him enthusiastic about kids and teaching. Please let my son also be a joy to that teacher. Thank you for all the dedicated, hard-working teachers who face my children every day in the classroom. Please give them the strength they need each day. In memory of the one who was called teacher *by his disciples. Amen.*

On Playing Peekaboo

Today I was in the supermarket line behind a young grandmother and a teenage mother with a baby in the shopping basket. They both ignored the baby while the groceries were being checked out. The baby, about a year and a half old, wept with the tired cry of babies who spend too much time in stores.

I caught the baby's eye from behind my mound of groceries, and without words, I played the time-honored game of peekaboo. While waiting for my grinning face to appear from behind the roll of paper towels, the baby broke into grins and laughter. We had five precious minutes together. Her loved ones never noticed.

Dear Jesus, you who loved a happy time with little ones, please help us not to drag our babies and toddlers through the shopping centers so much. Perhaps we shop too much and should stay home more and meet the needs of little ones. Help us to think of little ways to cheer and comfort. Help us to remember that all of the shopping plazas in the world can't provide the precious moments we spend with children. Amen.

On Beauty

Today I had lunch in one of the most beautiful homes I've ever seen. The lunch was delicious, served in a perfect atmosphere of tasteful, interior decoration that made me feel immediately at home. The hostess was lovely. She has the most perfect, long blond hair I've ever seen, a good figure, beautiful hands, and six wonderful children. She played the piano for us and sang. She had made many of the exquisite handcrafted items that decorated her home. The thirty women there were awestruck by each new talent exhibited by our hostess.

Dear God, that group of ladies did a lot of comparing today. I heard them muttering to each other. I definitely had a tendency to feel a little lumpy and to hide my ragged cuticles. Forgive me Lord for comparing my lot with hers.

Thank you for that beautiful home and the gracious hostess that shares her gifts with others. Thank you for the Christlike witness that comes to all who enter there. Now show me what I can offer others. Teach me how to make the most of the talents you've given me. In memory of Jesus who created all beauty and talents. Amen.

On Boys in the Living Room

There are seven boys in my living room. The average age is eleven and one-half. They are talking and laughing and they don't care what the furniture looks like.

Dear God, thank you that my boys and their friends feel perfectly comfortable in our living room in spite of our worn-out furniture. Thank you that they want to be here. Help me keep my priorities straight so that people will always be more important than furniture or rugs or houses. May people always enjoy coming here and help my influence to be positive and nurturing. In memory of him who entertained his friends while sitting on the rocks near the Jordan River. Amen.

On *Song of the South*

Today I saw the movie *Song of the South*. It's my favorite of the Walt Disney classics, with Uncle Remus and Brer Rabbit making life a musical. This movie is special to me because I saw it for the first time with my Dad, thirty years ago. Seeing it today brought a flood of memories of how special I felt going to the movies alone with my Dad.

Dear Heavenly Father, you know I've often wanted life to be more like a musical with "Mr. Bluebird on my shoulder" and Daddy by my side. Thank you for those moments in my memory book. Help me to understand your plan that causes change to come. In memory of your son who would have loved to go to Walt Disney movies with you. Amen.

On Waiting in the Doctor's Office

In the doctor's waiting room today a little three-year-old was exploring and touching, wiggling and talking—not doing anything wrong, just doing what comes naturally. The mother kept reprimanding her and telling her to sit still and stop it. The little girl tried grinning at her grandma, and the grandma scowled and shook her head.

Dear God, help us to offer better alternatives than sitting still—a book to read, a finger play or drawing a picture together. Don't let us forget that these little people are the greatest explorers and students in the world. Help us to teach them and join with them in creative times, even while waiting. In the memory of him who said we must become as little children to enter the kingdom of heaven. Amen.

On Different Lifestyles

My eleven-year-old son, Scott, has just taken a shower, washed his hair, put on clean school clothes, climbed in bed, and gone to sleep for the night.

Perhaps his habits are a bit unorthodox, but they are not hurting him or me or anybody else. He's just not wasting his time dressing in the morning.

Dear Jesus, thank you for Scott and the beautiful lesson I've just learned. Just because something has been done a certain way for years doesn't make it the only way. Thank you for Scott's creativity and my ability to see his creativity. Help me to remember this event when our lifestyles vary to a greater degree on bigger issues. Help me to remember that my way of doing things is not the only right way. Let me be tolerant of different hairstyles, clothes and ways of being. In memory of Jesus who hung around with an unconventional group of friends. Amen.

On Old Newspapers

Today I put my old newspapers out on the curb. Like a miracle they were picked up by a lady I know who fills up her van with newspapers and sells them, turning the profit over to Christian missions.

She comes to my street once a month, but every other day she is systematically covering the rest of town picking up papers.

Dear God, thank you for the lady who picks up papers. Let her feel your closeness as she is faithful in her task. She's helping me by taking my papers. She is serving our environment by getting those papers recycled. And some missionaries are able to get your message out because of the money she gives. What an example to me of the body of

Christ working with the other parts to get your work done! In memory of the one who is the head of the "Big Recycling Project." Amen.

On a Rusty Bumper

While sitting in a parking lot, my car bumper must have been bumped. The odd thing is that this bumper does not have a respectable dent like you would expect to see in an upstanding bumper that got hit. There is just a gaping, rusty hole where it happened. It is just plain rusted out like the rest of the car. Even the shiny chrome veneer couldn't hide the fact that it had lost its "bumper power."

Dear Heavenly Father, I have an uneasy feeling that there's a lesson here for me. Perhaps the bumpers of my soul are rusted out, too. Please make my bumpers strong enough in you so that I won't just be rusted out when hit with life's experiences. In memory of Jesus who warned us against rusty treasures. Amen.

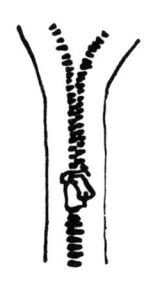

On Zippers

I've put in two zippers. One in a winter jacket, and last night, in a pair of boy's pants. My mother had done more than her share of installing zippers for me and I just decided to learn the job myself and let her have some other kind of fun in her golden years.

My fourteen year old found me at the sewing machine, putting in that zipper. "Isn't that hard?" he asked. "I thought it was Grandma's type of work." "It is, but every day I'm closer to being a Grandma," I answered. We laughed together and felt close and loving.

Dear God, thank you for zippers and other everyday things that help us find those fleeting seconds of intimacy and preciousness with our dear ones. In memory of him who lived before the days of zippers and buttons. Amen.

On a Funeral

Today I went to a funeral of a young mother who died of cancer. The room was filled with mothers who knew it might have been them. Yet, it was a celebration of a life lived in harmony with you—a life that was a testimony of faith in who you are and that was ready to be with you.

Dear God, losing a friend in death seems like a great price to pay, but thank you for reminding us that life on this earth has a limited number of days. If we don't get about your business now, we never will. Help us to savor the relationships with our loved ones. Thank you that days with you in heaven are limitless. In memory of Jesus, who wept when Lazarus died. Amen.

On Valentine's Day

Today is Valentine's Day. I went to the nursing home with my son Scott to take a bag of Valentines made by his fifth grade class. We talked to the people and admired the other cards their relatives had sent.

The evidence of festivities prompted me to comment to one lucid lady resident that it was nice that they were having some parties. She said yes, that *they* were entertaining the fifth grade class from the elementary school today.

Dear Lord, how wonderful that the lady had the idea that the residents were entertaining the visiting class. Her belief confirms my experience with nursing homes—I've gone many times to serve and always have found myself being served. In memory of the one who came to serve, not to be served. Amen.

On Three in a Bedroom

Tonight I looked at my three sons sleeping close together in their bedroom. I'm thankful that they get along so well they want to sleep together.

Dear Jesus, thank you that there really are not enough bedrooms so each can have his own. Help them to love and care for each other and appreciate being together. Forgive me for the times I think I need more space. I'm reminded that you often shared the ground with your twelve friends. Amen.

On Guna the Guinea Pig

Guna died today. He was a two-pound guinea pig who had been with us for two and a half years. How well I remember the day we got him. First we got Sneezy, and then a week later, Guna came to keep him company. To me, these pets were a necessary part of my children's lives as they grew up. The boys spent happy hours making a wooden cage and some weary hours arguing about who would clean it and feed the furry rodents. The cage is large, and I often eyed its corner in the utility room, thinking of the day Guna and Sneezy would be gone, and I could have that storage space.

Dear Lord, I was surprised at my own emotions when I heard those words, Guna died. *There was no mistaking the look of death in that stiff little body. I wept mostly for see-*

ing my brave and tender twelve year old digging the grave in the rich brown soil near the tomatoes. He said that he hoped that Guna had a happy life. I said I felt sure he did, and that he had given so much happiness to others. Twice I looked in that brown shopping bag at the furry body so done with life. I stood in awkward silence while that brown bag coffin was pressed into the hole and dirt packed down on top. The boys looked sad for a moment, then picked up the shovel and went on to other things. I had to be alone and cry for this experience was a vivid reminder that all of life on earth is temporary. In memory of him who died to give us eternal life. Amen.

On Husbands Who Stay Late at the Office

My husband is putting in more time at the office than at home. At least that's the way it seems. Today he said he knew of a man who stayed away from home a lot, because he felt pressure there. I gently asked him if that might also be his case. The answer came back, "Yes."

Dear Lord, in the context of our lives, how can I help but be synonymous with mortgage, debts and bills? Of course, he knows I have many needs. He knows I need his time and wish his time for our children. Lord, help me to find my sufficiency in you, so I will overflow with your spirit. Help me to be a giver not a taker, so my husband will come to me for refreshment and nourishment. Teach me to be beautiful in every way and to build him up, so he will feel his best. In the name of him who is the Bread of Life and the Living Water. Amen.

On a Hole in the Ceiling

Today my son Steve asked to cut a hole in the bedroom ceiling. Silly question? Yes, at first we thought so. Should we think of house resale value? Would it look bad? Is it permissive? Those were all necessary considerations. But after hearing his case, we let him do it. Space is cramped in a room shared by three boys. The attic would provide a getaway for Steve who wants a little privacy at age fourteen.

> *Dear Lord, the attic is wired for lights and carpeted with old rugs now, and the hole in the ceiling has a neat door with edging that matches the molding. It took a lot of work for Steve, and now his interests have changed. But thank you for the fun he had doing it and the appreciation he expressed for our saying yes when we had no real reason to*

say no. In memory of Our Father who has said yes so many times that we know there's a reason for those loving no's. Amen.

On a Thirty-fifth Wedding Anniversary

Today I worked in my neighbor's kitchen while she entertained for her parents' thirty-fifth wedding anniversary. It was a big open house, and I had fun washing the dishes and keeping the table filled with goodies for the buffet. I enjoyed the people so much. I felt like part of their family.

Dear Lord, thank you for simple kinds of service that invariably bring me more pleasure than I give. Thank you for houses full of loving friends and relatives. Help us to savor human beings at least as much as we do a beautiful sunset or a perfect rose. In the name of the Creator who made each person unique. Amen.

On Past and Future

The chair was green and overstuffed. I was four years old and four times a day by leaning over the back of that chair I could look out the window and watch the kids go to and from school.

I dreamed of the day I could enter that grownup world and be counted among those wise people who knew the secret adventures that went on in "school."

> *Dear God, most of my life I have spent looking forward to events—school, dating, marriage, babies. Now I'm starting to look back on many things. Please help me learn to live completely in the present moment, since the past is over and tomorrow is in your hands. In memory of the one who is the beginning and the end. Amen.*

On Being an Optimist or a Complainer

I'm at my desk again, daydreaming, hardly moving papers from the "in" box to the "out" box. I just read something in a paper from my home town that got me on the memory train of my childhood. The box cars of that train are my home, my school, my friends, and my neighborhood. As a child, there was no room in my mind for any challenge of the indisputable fact that "mine" were the best!

The thing I just realized with horror, is that now that I am middle-aged, I've changed. My circumstances are just a little different—now I am a mother, not a daughter; but the sad truth and the greatest difference is that once I was an optimist, and now I'm a complainer.

Dear God, forgive me. I weep in remorse for what has just been revealed to me. I remember as a child that I was so in love with life and everything around me. Now my attitude seems different. Too often I gripe about my home, my children's schools, my husband's schedule. What a destructive habit! Please let me be one who builds up, not one who is negative. In the name of him who promised the abundant life. Amen.

On Desk Work

There are insurance forms to fill out, bills to pay, sympathy letters to write, notes of congratulations, and letters of recommendation. My whole life seems to flash before me as I work at my desk on this combination of mundane business tasks and personal touches with human beings.

Lord, you know I push the papers back and forth, dust the desk, and get a bite to eat. I clean the drawers and find old letters that make me laugh and cry and daydream. Yet this work must be done, and I must get on with other tasks. Let me learn to dispatch these chores efficiently, so that I can get on with other things. Remind me of the importance of little notes that encourage people as they experience the milestones of life. Let those never be a burden. In the name of the Living Word. Amen.

On April Fool's Day

Today is April Fool's Day. I called my Dad and told him there were pink elephants in our back yard. This has been our tradition for the last thirty-five years, and we treat those pachyderms with mock-seriousness.

Dear Lord, how I love the predictability of long-term, loving relationships! I want April Fool's Day to always be the same—my Dad and I talking about the pink elephants in the backyard. I want the good parts of life, like the people I love, to always be with me. I don't like the way things have to change. Help me to understand and to accept the changes as a part of life. In memory of the one who is always with us. Amen.

On BankAmericard

It's 3:00 A.M. I'm at my desk, paying bills to Master Charge and BankAmericard, because I can't sleep. The little fears and worries are magnified by the darkness and the quiet, so I pass the time paying bills and doing other business chores.

Dear Lord, thank you for the gift of time. When anxiety swallows up sleep, help me to use well the bonus waking hours to accomplish tasks that need to be done. As though elves have been here, my family notices the desk is cleaner in the morning than it was the night before. But more important, let me not forget to give you time to clean the cobwebs from my heart. In memory of him, who left his mark without a desk and paid his bills without BankAmericard. Amen.

On Going to Graduate School

Today in conversation, I said, "I'm going to go to graduate school." The people were impressed. It made me feel so important.

Dear God, I'm not fooling you. I have other "gods before you." How subtle are these things we worship. Education is a wonderful thing, until it becomes my God. While I'm at it, I might as well confess, because you already know of other idols that I've had—houses, clothes, and fun times. Forgive me, please—again. Amen.

On Quitting Graduate School

Today I decided not to get a Masters Degree. I'm currently taking my first graduate school course. I enjoy it, and I'm learning, but study time takes too much time away from my family.

Dear God, I had to take that course to find out. If I hadn't, I always would have wondered. I'm sure I've been influenced by women I know who say they are fulfilled getting their Masters or Ph.D. I'm glad there are so many kinds of people in the world. Thank you for making me the kind of woman who is fulfilled being a mommy. In memory of Jesus, whose mother never went to college. Amen.

On Senility

Today I visited a lady in the nursing home who doesn't remember me or respond at all. For five years she hasn't seemed to recognize her husband or any of their friends. When I speak to her, I tell her about mutual acquaintances and what I think would interest her if she were not so senile. No matter what I say or do, she just stares at me as if she's not hearing a thing.

Dear God, thank you that you are responsible for the results of our ministries of love. If I only went to the nursing home to see results or response, I would have quit going long ago. Thank you that my part is to be faithful in the tasks you've asked me to do. In memory of the one who has waited a long time for our response to his love. Amen.

On Waiting My Turn

My husband just came home from a convention, and, as is typical of me, I'm eager to ask him who he saw that I know. After a quick kiss and hello, my fourteen-year-old son barraged him with questions about electronics, and they are into that subject in a big way this very minute.

So, Lord, I'm back at my desk, which isn't as much fun as hearing about people and events. Once you said, "in everything give thanks." I am thankful for a son who has a keen mind that thinks up questions about electronics and a husband who loves to share the answers with him. Lord, it's good to know that my son is with his dad. My turn will be soon. Thank you for that assurance. In memory of the one who continually waits for us. Amen.

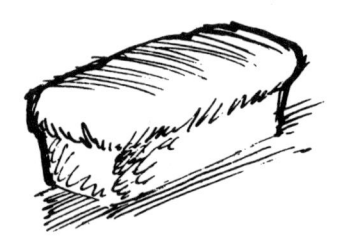

On Homemade Limpa Bread

An eighty-year-old relative was buried today. After the funeral service and procession to the cemetery, there was a luncheon served at the daughter's home. While going through the buffet line, I tried to make small talk with one of the teenage granddaughters. "What a beautiful variety of breads," I said. "That's Grandma's last homemade Limpa and Swedish coffee bread," she answered.

I felt the impact of what she had said. Her grandmother had baked the bread that was being eaten at her own funeral luncheon. Of course when she was busily mixing the ingredients, she assumed she would be alive to enjoy the finished product with her loved ones. Not only did she bake bread for all of us, but she sang in church just hours before she died.

Dear Heavenly Father, thank you for this woman who was busy right up to her last hours on earth. Thank you that she sang for you and baked bread for us just before walking through Heaven's door. Please help me to be useful and full of zest for life right up to the moment you call me home. In memory of the one who has prepared mansions for us. Amen.

On Bike Riding and Jealousy

I just got back from my "after supper" bike ride. My son's second-hand bike with the coaster brakes is what I ride. When I learned to ride a bike in the 1940s, there were no three speeds or ten speeds with hand brakes, so the familiar foot brakes suit me just fine.

I'm one of those middle-aged ladies in Bermuda shorts who goes slowly around the block to get in shape. I love the fun and exercise and the feeling of the air rushing by. I'm watching the progress of a beautiful house some friends are building.

There I go again, Lord. I'm half way interested in that house, one fourth happy for my friends and one fourth jealous. Will I always have this problem? Is this human nature that the grass always seems to be greener on the other side of the fence? I know covetousness is common to all humanity but why can't I, since I belong to you, transcend this sin more often than I do? Perhaps the answer is, that being such a sinner keeps me coming back to you for forgiveness. Please, Lord, forgive me once again, and thank you that you've said you will and do. Amen.

... ANYBODY?

On Listening

A tiny voice comes from the bedroom upstairs: "Steve, Dave, Scott . . . anybody." It sounds so distant, like a person locked in the closet. In reality it's the boy next door coming through on a speaker system from his house to our boys' bedroom. With speakers, microphones and copper wire, the boys spent hours making this set-up. It's lost its novelty now, but even when my own boys are out playing, I sometimes hear that little voice calling earnestly for "anybody who will listen."

Dear God, please let me always be attentive to those around me who just need "someone" to listen. The "little voice" has reminded me to be aware of all around me who need a listening ear. But don't let me neglect the obvious, that little voice of the twelve-year-old boy next door. In memory of the one who always hears us when we call. Amen.

On Old-Timers

While waiting for people to assemble at a funeral today, I shook hands with the eighty-year-old brother of the deceased. Inside I cried for this dear man whose friends and relatives are leaving him alone, with hardly any peers. "Seven old-timers have died in the last two weeks," he said. "At my age, it's hard to make friends. The young folks don't want to take time for old people."

Dear God, help me to take time to be a friend to those who most need friends. Don't let me forget the old folks who are so lonely and have so much to share. Please let there be some thoughtful young people around me when I am eighty. In memory of Jesus who loves the old-timers. Amen.

On Buying a House

Should I have bought the other house? It had more space and was cheaper; but it was in bad repair. On the other hand, with a little loving care, it might have been quite nice. Or, it might have caused a lot of trouble and required a lot of money to fix up. But still, I can't get it out of my mind. It sneaks into my thoughts in the middle of the night when I'm trying to figure out how to cut back on living expenses.

Dear Jesus, I remember that you said you give your kind of peace—not like the peace the world provides. I claim your peace right now. I need to get some closure on this decision that was made and is now "water under the bridge." I hear others say that you clearly lead them to the right decision, and they feel so good about it. I'm not quick to say, "God showed me this," or "taught me that," or "wanted me to buy this house." You know my own confusion enters in, and I do not always know your will. Please give me your peace in decision-making. Let me move forward in your paths. In memory of the one whose word is a lamp for my feet and a light for my path. Amen.

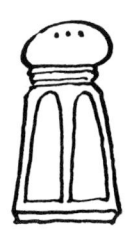

On the Salt of the Earth

Someone said that this is not a friendly town. I am amazed, because I've found it very friendly. People are so important in my life. I enjoy giving coffee parties for new neighbors, even if I'm new in town myself. I want to be the salt of the earth in my contacts with people. I want to provide the seasoning that helps make life taste good.

Dear God, you did not suggest I be the salt of the earth, nor did you say to try it for a while. You simply said, "You are the salt of the earth." Please help me to remember that salt spread around is good; that too much salt is bad. Perhaps if I learn the balance between hiding my light or com-

ing on too strong, I can help this place be known as a "friendly" town. In memory of the one who was known as the friendly carpenter in his neighborhood. Amen.

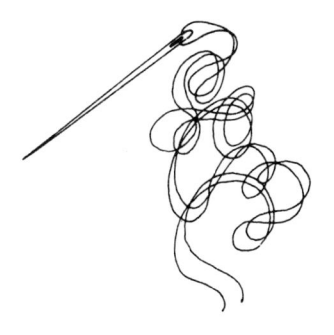

On Learning from Mistakes

Today I threw away some half-finished needlework. I had made some bad mistakes on the stitches and the use of colors. I tried to fix it but I couldn't. I thought of selling it in a garage sale but knew no one would buy it. Finally, I decided that I had learned from the experience and would do much better next time.

Dear Heavenly Father, I've made a lot of mistakes with cakes and pies and sewing. I often have to say I'm sorry to friends and family. I don't mind the times I've messed up hanging wallpaper or painting window trim, but please let me not make mistakes that cause pain in people's lives. In memory of him who forgives my mistakes. Amen.

On an Escaped Hamster

Our hamster escaped from his cage. He got between the walls and every night about ten o'clock he started chewing his way through the wall. He chewed and scratched until about seven o'clock in the morning, rested for the day, and then started in at night. The escape route he chose was right beside our bed, and the gnawing went on for a week. Finally, after an all-night vigil, his teeth and nose came into view, and my husband caught the little critter as he popped through the opening and into his hand. We moved a dresser in front of the hole.

Dear God, sometimes I get myself stuck between walls. I work my way through slowly just like the hamster, and you are always waiting patiently for me. In memory of the one who told the story of the waiting father. Amen.

On Babies Who Grow Up

In little ways I see it—my baby is a man. Mommies are the last to notice. When I kiss my fifteen-year-old son (which is only when no one else will see, since he's not much for kissing), I still remember graham crackers stuck between his chins.

Now he's all lean and hard and muscular, and stronger than I. He knows far more than I about space and mechanical things and what clothes look best on him.

Dear God, help me to recognize that most of my work with my son is done. Thank you for the beautiful results, which are really your doing. Help me to know my place, to be accepting and supportive, and to realize that to build a man for you was the whole idea when he was born. It's hard, but teach me how to loosen my hold and turn him over to you. In memory of him who wandered off from his folks in the temple in Jerusalem. Amen.

On a Box of Kleenex

Today I noticed a box of Kleenex in the home of a friend. It was a fancy blue one, with flowers on it, and it was a perfect touch to the beautiful decor. I noticed that box of Kleenex because I have one at home just like it, but mine doesn't look half as good. I just don't seem to have the knack of making a room look like a picture in *Better Homes and Gardens*. Seeing that beautiful home got me all hung-up on "things" again.

Dear Jesus, forgive me for the sin of coveting. I think too much about shag rugs, family rooms and sliding glass patio doors. Remind me that the abundant life involves the fruits of the spirit, not formal dining rooms, custom made drapes, and color coordinated furniture. In memory of the Man of Nazareth who knew how to keep his priorities straight. Amen.

On Monster Mutant Bikes

Today there are nine bikes in my garage. No car could enter there—no space for such an intruder. These bikes are not ten-speeds or three-speeds or even bikes with all their parts. They are really junk bikes. Old frames are easily found in dumps and with a few old wheels, a castoff handle bar, and maybe a taped up seat, these monster mutant bikes become workable vehicles. Some look very strange. One is termed "the heap." There is one I really like and call my own, risking each day that when I go to ride it the handlebars or seat may be different. They rarely stay the same. These amazing bikes are assembled by a half dozen eleven-to-fifteen-year-old mechanics.

Dear God, I loved it when my preschool boys made creations out of Tinker Toys. What carry-over value that ac-

tivity had! Now help me to enjoy the grease and clutter and noise, because someday the funny bikes will all be gone as surely as the Tinker Toys are gone. And I will yearn for the days I watched a baby or a boy work on his own creation. In memory of the one who used his creative talents to put the stars in place. Amen.

On Old Hymns

I heard some beautiful old hymns today on the radio. Flooding back into my mind came the old-fashioned hymn-sings of my childhood, the church-camp vespers of twenty-five years ago, the Sunday night youth group all bringing heaven right into my experience. The old favorites are tied in with precious memories, and yet, they give me a window to heaven.

Dear Jesus, more than sermons and Sunday school, the singing makes me feel close to you. It's like the roof will lift, and heaven will be there instead. I feel my heart will break or my lungs will burst, the singing makes you seem so near. Since I was a little child, I've held the secret belief that the corridor from this life to the next will be filled with all those I've loved, singing the grand old hymns. If it be Thy will. Amen.